Laugh and Live: Humor for Humans

Kellen Brooks

Copyright © 2025 Kellen Brooks

All rights reserved.

Paperback
ISBN: 978-0-9888030-6-0

E-book
ISBN: 978-0-9888030-5-3

Laugh and Live: Humor for Humans

Copyright © 2025 Kellen Brooks

All rights reserved. This book of any portion thereof may not be reproduced or used in any manner whatsoever without the express written permission of the publisher except for the use of brief quotations.

First Printing: 2025

Order Information: For details on bulk purchases, please contact the publisher at KellenBrooks.com

Laugh and Live: Humor for Humans

Dedication

This book is dedicated to Isaac King, Jr. and Charles Pratt: men that showed me the beauty, divinity, and healing power of laughter.
(Proverbs 17:22)

CONTENTS

	Dedication	iv
	Foreword	vii
	Before You Read	xi
1	Animal Humor	1
2	Food Humor	11
3	Music Humor	21
4	Religious Humor	29
5	Dating Humor	35
6	Cultural Humor	41
7	Finance Humor	45
8	Dark-ish Humor	49

9 Snowman Humor 51

10 Sports Humor 55

11 A Little Bit of Everything: Cars, Alphabet, Political, and Random Humor 57

11 Witty "Wisdom" 71

FOREWORD

They say laughter is the best medicine. If that's true, then Pastor Kellen Brooks is a pharmacist… without the white coat, but with a pen and paper.

I've been blessed to serve as a Christian comedian for many years, and I've seen first-hand that laughter can do what nothing else can. I've watched a room full of strangers turn into a family in under five minutes because of humor. I've seen people walk into a show carrying the weight of the world and leave lighter — not because their circumstances changed, but because their perspective did.

Laugh and Live: Humor for Humans

Science agrees with me on this one. There are studies showing that patients heal faster when comedians are brought into hospitals. Their pain decreases. Their spirits lift. Their bodies actually respond better to treatment. Now, I'm not saying we should replace doctors with Pastor Kellens' "What do you call an…" — though it would make waiting rooms a whole lot more interesting — but I am saying that joy does something powerful in the human heart.

The Bible said it first: "A cheerful heart is good medicine" (Proverbs 17:22). Laughter doesn't just tickle us — it touches something eternal inside of us. It's as if God hardwired our souls to need joy, and when we laugh, we're reminding ourselves that hope is still alive and well.

That's exactly what happened to me the first time I came across Pastor Kellens' "one liners" on Facebook. Now, I've seen a lot of social media content in my day. Some of it's funny, some of it's not, and some of it makes you want to throw your phone in the middle of the street, during rush hour traffic… in Atlanta!! But Pastor Kellen's posts were

Laugh and Live: Humor for Humans

different.

They were short, witty, and clever — the kind of humor that makes you stop scrolling, chuckle out loud, and think, "Now that was good." I'd be in the middle of a busy day, maybe on my way to a meeting or even Sunday morning service, and I'd see one of his posts. Instantly, I'd feel a little lighter. Sometimes it was a quick grin, but it did the job!

It's amazing how something so simple can be so impactful. Those "one liners" weren't just random thoughts — they were little gifts of joy, sprinkled into the timeline chaos. They didn't ask for your time, but they gave you a moment you didn't know you needed. And now… there's a whole book of them.

Let me tell you, I'm excited about this book. Not just because it's funny — though it absolutely is — but because it's a collection of moments that remind us how powerful laughter can be. Every page is an opportunity to smile, to exhale, and to remember that no matter what's going on in the world, there's

Laugh and Live: Humor for Humans

still something worth laughing about.

That's what Pastor Kellen has done here. He's bottled up joy, wrapped it in wit, and handed it to us like medicine — the kind you don't dread taking. This isn't just making us laugh; it's about connection, perspective, and the reminder that God's people can have a good time and still be holy.

In a world that seems determined to keep us stressed, divided, and on edge, this book is a breath of fresh air. So as you turn these pages, don't just read them — let them do their work. Let them lift your spirit, loosen your shoulders, and maybe even make latterly laugh out loud!

Pastor Kellen, thank you for reminding us that humor is holy, joy is a gift, and laughter might just be the closest thing we have to a universal language. To everyone else holding this book — prepare yourself. The doctor is in, the prescription is joy, and the refill is unlimited.

Now, take a deep breath… and enjoy.

– Pastor Tirrell McCoy

BEFORE YOU READ

All the humor in this book is clean humor, digestible for all audiences. However, it is written with adults in mind. You may find some of the contents not be suitable (or even understandable) for younger audiences. Laughter is human, so let your hair down and enjoy!
– Kellen Brooks

1
ANIMAL HUMOR

Q: What do you call an overweight Christmas tree?
A: A Porky-Pine.

Q: A lamb wrote a stage play about relationships?
A: It's called "Why good girls like baaad boys"

Q: Why did the panda get knee replacements?
A: It couldn't bear the weight.

Animal Humor

Q: What bird barbecues the best?
A: Flaming-os!

Q: Which birds don't have many friends?
A: The ones that are ostrich-ized.

Q: What do you call an overweight bird?
A: Robin Thick.

Q: Name a bird that hates Black History Month?
A: A Jim Crow.

Q: Why are sharks so spiritual?
A: They prey a lot.

Q: What word describes a pig's fashion sense?
A: Pig Sty-le

Q: What do you call 2 pigs hugging?
A: A ham sandwich.

Q: Why did the all star pig's basketball season end?
A: Because it pulled pork.

Q: Why do pigs delay marriage?
A: They have too many ribs to choose from.

Q: Who won the fight between the horse and Lion?
A: The horse. He can buck!

Animal Humor

Q: What's a horse's favorite dance?
A: The neigh neigh.

Q: Where do cows evangelize?
A: The utter-most parts of the world.

Q: Why can't bulls make friends?
A: They're always having run-ins.

Q: Why do bulls dress so nice?
A: They shop at Target.

Q: What's the holiest bird out there?
A: A cardinal.

Q: What bird always needs cheering up?
A: A bluejay.

Q: How would Jonah describe being in the Whale's belly?
A: It dampened his mood.

Q: What word describes a pig's fashion sense?
A: Pig sty-le.

Q: What caused the leopard's black spots?
A: Jungle fever.

Q: I know a wealthy lamb.
A: He's got racks.

Q: How do you protect a goose from being hunted?
A: Yell, "Duck! Duck!"

Animal Humor

Q: What animal tells the worst jokes?
A: A Uni-corny.

Q: The fisherman downsized his boat
A: He now rides a lil yachty.

Q: Did you know frogs love gospel music?
A: Their favorite artist is Tye 'Ribbett.

Q: What product do snakes use to clean their house?
A: Serpentine.

Q: Why don't sheep like to loan money?
A: They're always getting fleeced.

Q: Why are birds the best dressed animals?
A: Because they stay fly.

Q: What animal was arrested for stealing?
A: The octopus. It had hands everywhere!

Q: Why are grizzlies the most affectionate animals?
A: Because they give bear hugs.

Q: What's a nursery rhyme for folks who talk too much:
A: Blah blah black sheep.

Q: Why should you always perfume your turkey during the holidays?
A: To get rid of the fowl odor.

Animal Humor

Q: What's better than one bird?
A: Cockatwo.

Q: What do you call an offensive bird?
A: Flagrant Fowl

Q: Why shouldn't you take financial advice from bulls?
A: Because they charge everything.

This rooster tried to mimic a robin and stand on a power line. Needless to say, he's fried chicken now. –Tré Harris

The horse across the street shovel my snow. He's a good neigh-bor.

If you want the hard truth, talk to a fisherman. They always keep it reel.

Kellen Brooks

The "Justice for Marine Animals" corporation has chosen a theme song for the year. Seashell overcome.

I enrolled my dog in therapy. He's been having a ruff time lately.

I have a pet parrot named Lawrence. His nick name is Larry Bird.

A kangaroo has been working hard at the gym doing sit ups. It can't seem to get rid of its pouch though.

Some asked me what to name their pet. I said "Name him Elvis. He's nothing but a hound dog."

A bee stung me the other day. It didn't live to tell about it.

Leopards hate math. They run away from their problems.

2
FOOD HUMOR

Q: What did the mosquito say when it bit a black person?
A: "Yum! Dark meat."

I met the sweetest and happiest cattleman on the farm the other day. He's a jolly rancher.

The detective said birds can be sneaky. Especially sparrows. His eyes are on the sparrow.

Kellen Brooks

My pet turtle loves Mexican food, especially hard shell tacos.

A doe charged at me and all I could think was, "Oh Deer!"

Q: Where is the best place for a tired chicken?
A: A bed of rice.

Q: What do you call a Little Debbie© fresh out of the oven?
A: A hot girl.

Q: What kind of meal is eaten while walking?
A: A tread-meal.

Q: Why are some chefs mediocre?
A: Because they cook medium well.

Food Humor

Q: What vegetable is a great musical producer?
A: Beets.

Q: What did the layer cake say to the pound cake?
A: It's time to level up.

Q: Why are some foods afraid to be thrown on the grill?
A: Cause' they don't want this smoke!

Q: What's the best way to Spice up your tailgate food
A: Football season-ing.

Q: What TV show gave Mr. Potato Head nightmares?
A: M.A.S.H.

Q: What vegetable does every driver need in their car?
A: A-spare-I-guess.

Q: Who won the beans vs. cornbread fight?
A: Cornbread. It gave beans a black eye.

Q: Did you see the boxing match between the carrot and the strawberry?
A. Strawberry won with a fruit punch!

Q: Did you know that pigs are incredible musicians?
A: They have all the musical chops.

Q: What racist soup should be banned?
A: Klan-chowder.

Food Humor

Q: Did you know that cider mills are big business?
A: As they say, apple pays!

Q: Did you hear there's a new bakery in Detroit?
A: It's called "What up dough!?"

Q: What's an arrogant person's favorite breakfast food?
A: Ego Waffles.

Q: What do beverage do people with integrity drink?
A: Genuine draft.

Q: Why did the bomb squad show up to the barbecue?
A: Because someone blew up the bathroom.

Q: Why don't turkeys go to potlucks?
A: Because it cost them their lives.

Q: What kind of dessert do you give your enemy to end a feud?
A: A peace cobbler.

Q: What's the funniest sandwich you can eat?
A: A comedy club.

Q: What did peanut butter dance to at the wedding?
A: Slow Jams.

Q: What TV should you never watch during a tummy ache?
A: I Love Loosey.

Food Humor

Q: Why should you never row your boat in the kitchen?
A: Because the kitchen sinks.

Q: At what age do you start getting constipated?
A: Blockage.

Q: What's the fatest city in Texas?
A: Corpulent Cristi.

Q: How do you fix broken Tupperware?
A: Plastic surgery.

Q: What item in your kitchen would win a fashion show?
A: The faucet. It's got the drip.

Kellen Brooks

Q: What do you call a mushroom who doesn't like to have fun?
A: No funGus.

I don't like people around while I'm having a grilled cheese sandwich. I prefer to eat it provalone.

Frog legs are my favorite food. I leap for joy every time I eat them.

It seems like the food coloring has lost its will to live. It keeps saying "Let me dye!"

I started using a ketchup flavored mouthwash. It's called condiment.

Grapes have it bad. They get crushed and bruised for wine and juice. But their hardest job is raisin kids.

Food Humor

Never eat when your mad or else you'll have an upset stomach!

I saw a guy rob a bakery. He said it was a piece of cake.

I saw a drunk traffic officer the other day. Turns out, he was drinking Patrol.

If you really want to get your wife to cook for you, buy her a dozen flours and 24 carrots.

I once had a friend named Biscuit. He was flaky.

You can never go wrong with Chinese food, especially when it's fried right.

I had a bread joke to tell you, but it was stale.

Kellen Brooks

I talk quietly during dinner, but ice cream for dessert.

I would travel to Greece for vacation, but it's not good for my cholesterol.

Church's chicken is broadening their family of restaurants with their latest addition, Synagogue Subs.

Barista's love to gossip, I'm told. They spill the tea.

The fortune cookies irony is it couldn't predict it would live a broken life.

Sally is embarrassed to eat omelettes in front of people. She always gets egg on her face.

Pizza is pizza, no matter how you slice it.

Food Humor

I keep one drinking glass in my cabinet. It's a solo cup.

A chef decided to give curry a shot to season his food. Now he can't stop making three course meals.

I enjoy the bright flavor of sun flower seeds. Very light!

There is a new restaurant that's ran completely by AI. They use a lot of artificial flavoring.

3
MUSIC HUMOR

Q: What's is the Lumberjacks' favorite gospel song?
A: Stump.

Q: What's a coal miners favorite music artist?
A: Coaltrane.

Q: What did Batman name his firstborn son?
A: Lil' Wayne.

Music Humor

Q: Why did Mickey Mouse fire the DJ at Minnie Mouse's birthday party?
A: He kept playing trap music.

Q: What song did Noah play on repeat through the flood?
A: When Doves Cry.

Q: Abstinent people hate to travel here.
A: Californication.

Q: What's a porcupine's favorite rap song?
A: We Stay on Point Like Stacy Adams.

Q: Name that gospel singer who played for the Dallas Mavericks
A: Dirk Franklin.

Q: What's Country singing group stinks?
A: Brooks and Dung.

Q: What's better than two songs?
A: Tres Songz.

Q: What's a marathoners favorite music to listen to?
A: Miles Davis.

Q: How much did Jay-Z tip his server?
A: $4.44.

Q: Why did everyone drop out of Algebra class?
A: They didn't want these problems.

Music Humor

Q: What do you call an orchestra conductor's only child?
A: Unison.

They just released the theme song for the national archery competition. Throw Dem Bows.

The whole world should become a choir. That way, we could live in harmony.

Spiderman is starting a rap career. His stage name is Silk the Shocker.

The royal family enjoys the music of Prince, particularly Purple Reign.

My new house plant has great musical taste. It really enjoys The Roots.

I like to play smooth jazz when I'm on rough roads.

Hip Hop artist are very green. They recycle plastic wrap.

A Musical ABC Story

I had a vacation planned for Canada and instead of taking a plane, I took The **A-Train**. I put on my headphones to listen to **Be-bop** but decided to play **Cee-lo** instead. I arrived at my destination at the train station and the overhead speakers played **D-Nice.** It was like a party in there! I saw a sign that said "Rideshare pick up at gate **E-40**" so I made my way there. My driver arrived and when I got in the car he was blasting **FTP**, then **G-Unit.** Shocked by the music choices, I kindly asked that he play something a little more relaxing, like **RH Factor.**

He asked, "How about **iCarly**?"

I said, "Am I a child?"

He laughed and asked, "What about **Jay-Z**?"

Finally, I said, "Let's just shuffle some music."

Music Humor

I was surprised at what came on next! **K-Pop, Elle, Eminem**, then **N-Sync**. It was like time travel to the early 2000s! I finally made it to my hotel, dropped my bags and went to a baseball game. They opened the game with the national anthem **"O Canada."** The crowd became lively when the arena disc jockey started playing **PFunk** and **Q-tip**.

Next up at base was a slugger. He hit a home run and the ball seemed to soar to the moon and all of a sudden, they started playing **R Kelly** "I believe I can fly!"

It was 90s karaoke night at the baseball game, so they played **SUV** on the big screen for the sing-a-long. The seventh inning stretch was sung by **T-Pain**

The baseball game ended with a special concert by **U2** and we all held our cell phone flash lights in the air. **V** from BTS was there and performed some of the group hits.

I left the game and decided to walk. I saw a large party happening at a nearby venue, with the music blaring into the streets. I went in and saw that **W&W** was performing and mixing up some classics. The crowd went wild when they called up their special guest artist, **Xzibit,** to come on stage. He paid homage to **DMX** to start off the set. I cried crocodile tears, it was so special.

The night was getting late, so on my way to the hotel, I saw a church holding a night service. I thought, I can't go to a party and not go to church! I went inside and the preacher was singing the old song **Why Me?** A little tear came to my eye and I thanked God for a great weekend. I finally made it back to my room and before catching some zzz's I ended the night with some **ZZ Top**. What a day!

4
RELIGIOUS HUMOR

Q: What do you call a person that's been baptized twice?
A: Double-dipped.

Q: How many church mothers does it take to change a light bulb?
A: Two. One to "Loose it" and one to "Let it go"

Q: How come you shouldn't tell Judas your secrets?
A: He spills his guts to others.

Q: What did Joseph the dreamer wear on picture day?
A: A Coogi Sweater.

Q: What song got Noah through the flood?
A: When Doves Cry.

Q: Joseph bought Mary a cell phone. What company did he use?
A: Virgin Mobile©.

Q: What's the best place for computers to serve in church?
A: Mother Board.

Q: How could one describe Jonah's three days in the Whale's belly?
A: It dampened his mood.

Religious Humor

Q: Did you know that rank sinners are born in October?
A: It's a result of the Fall.

Q: What's Mary and Martha's favorite paintings?
A: Mary's favorite is the Crying Clown. Martha's favorite is the Moan-a Lisa.

Q: What's the only acceptable way to greet the devil?
A: Hell-O.

I went to a church that had cup holders in the seats. But we were only allowed to drink Shirley Temples.

Delilah broke her phone. It was a Samson-g.

Kellen Brooks

My antique grandfather clock finally died. It was just his time.

A photographer had a near-death experience. His life flashed before his eyes.

I saw man crying while driving an 18 wheeler. I asked why his heart was heavy and he said "he's been carrying a truck load lately."

Heaven Humor…

Someone asked me "Will there be steak in Heaven?"
I said, "Yes, but only if it's well done."

Someone asked me "Will there be donuts in Heaven?"
I said, "Yes, but only the holey ones."

Someone asked me "Will there be chicken in Heaven?"
I said, "Yes…but only wings."

Religious Humor

Somebody asked me, "Will there be dogs in Heaven?"

I said, "Yes, but they'll have a ruff time getting in."

5
DATING HUMOR

Q: What's the most tempting day to go on a date?
A: Thirst-day.

Q: If a girl acts like a baby what do you do?
A: Pacifier.

Q: What did the fingers say to the palm?
A: You're handsome.

Religious Humor

Q: What's a single person's favorite Tyler Perry movie?
A: "I can do bed all by myself."

Q: Why do forks marry spoons?
A: Because knives be cuttin' up!

Q: Why should you date a man that wears suspenders and a belt at the same time?
A: He is very secure.

Q: What do you call a gymnast that bounces around from girl to girl?
A: A tramp-oline.

Q: What letter has the most relationship trouble?
A: The one with all the X's.

Q: What game does a polygamist hate to play?
A: Uno.

Q: Why do girls with weave make the best landlords?
A: They grant extensions.

Q: How does a groom loosen up his outfit for the wedding?
A: He un-tux his shirt.

If you can, marry a girl named A-e-i-o-u-y. She keeps her vowels.

"Marry a vegetarian," They said. "They'll never have beef with you!"

I performed a wedding for two body builders. Something tells me they're going to have a strong marriage.

Religious Humor

I set my friend up on a blind date and she asked me to describe the guy. I told her he has good character and he's funny too. I guess you could say he's a stand up comic.

I was gonna tell a sexist joke, but only the girls would get it.

A lady started a trend wearing helmets for fashion. She's ahead of the curve I'd say.

"I once dated" humor…for him

I once dated a girl named Mercedes. She was high maintenance.

I once dated a girl named Porsche. She drove me away quickly.

I once dated a girl named October. She kept falling for other guys.

I once dated a girl name VCR. She moved forward too fast.

I once dated a girl named Rose. I picked her and she pricked me.

I once dated a girl named Heaven Lee Host. She kept me saved.

I once dated an undertaker. She let me down slowly.

"I once dated" humor…for her

I once dated a CEO. He kept bossing me around.

I once dated a police officer. He didn't warrant a second date.

I once dated a bird watcher. He struggled to keep his eyes on me.

Religious Humor

I once dated a body builder. He came on too strong.

I once dated a gardener. I picked the right one!

I once dated a race car driver. He drove me in circles.

6
CULTURAL HUMOR

Q: What's a black pilots favorite reading material?
A: Jet Magazine.

Q: What do you call a tattoo on the wrist?
A: A Time stamp.

There's a new razor line called Risky. It cuts really close.

Q: What is a Victoria's secret model too proud to admit?
A: She is freezing.

Cultural Humor

I have a friend who's half Egyptian and half Irish. His name is CleoPatrick.

I went to Paris and saw an eye full!

Soviet's tend to be late. They're always Russian somewhere.

I hired a Jewish Uber driver the other day. He's my new shofar.

I went to New York to see the Statue of Liberty. It didn't move me. Then I remembered, statues don't move.

I just found out who got the leading role in Cars 4. Wheel Smith.

I have a friend who does somersaults all the time. We call him Flip-pé.

Kellen Brooks

There's a new clothing line that will get you blacklisted if you wear it. It's called Cancel Couture.

Just found out Jet Li and another famous Lee had the same father. A Parent Lee.

Cultural Humor

7
FINANCE HUMOR

Q: How did the crooked Pharaoh make his money?
A: Pyramid Schemes.

Q: Why are bulls terrible money managers?
A: Because they charge everything.

Q: Why don't cows loan money?
A: They're always getting milked.

Finance Humor

Q: What shouldn't you loan money to a corn stalk

A: Because it shucks and jives when it's time to pay up.

Q: What's a thief's favorite shoe?

A: Steal-toe boots.

Q: What was Superman's worst financial investment?

A: Krypto currency.

Q: Who's the wealthiest supermodel?

A: Tyra. She banks.

We're suing the city for false advertisement. They make us pay tolls on the freeway.

Kellen Brooks

My bank keeps inviting me to parties every weekend. They said I have insufficient fun.

I saw a man that went bankrupt. All I could think was, "Poor guy."

I always order extra starch at the dry cleaners, but it costs me so much bread!

I bought a plane ticket and the price was sky high. I guess that means I'll be riding submarines from now on. The price is so low.

I always catch gross fish when I use a net.

Balloons are more expensive than ever. It's because of inflation.

Finance Humor

8
DARK-ISH HUMOR

Q: What's a Ghosts favorite fruit?
A: Boo-berry.

Q: Why did the undertaker need a cough drop?
A: He's always coffin.

Q: Where do Ghosts buy their clothes from?
A: The Boo-tique.

Dark-ish Humor

Q: What's a ghost's favorite music?
A: R&B, Rhythm & Boo!

I was going to tell you a ghost joke, but I don't wanna get boo'd.

Ghost always has a boyfriend. She stays boo'd up.

The local funeral home is hiring drummers to play their graveyard services. Deadbeats only.

A cyclists are prepared if they ever passes away. They all have two wills.

Q: What channel only plays scary movies?
A: Net-flinch.

Q: At what age do you stop being afraid?
A: Cour-age.

9
SNOWMAN HUMOR

Q: What kind of person do Snowmen fall in love with?
A: The one that gives them the cold shoulder.

Q: Why are snowmen are the hardest working employees?
A: Because getting fired would kill them.

Q: Why did the snowman get food poisoning?
A: He ate a patty melt.

Snowman Humor

Q: When do snowboys become snowmen?
A: When they're tired of being flakes.

Q: What's a gender neutral term for a snowman?
A: There's snow such name.

Q: Why doesn't a snowman ever lose?
A: Because he is made in the win-ter.

Q: Did you know snowmen are banned from donating blood?
A: They have ice in their veins.

Q: What's a snowman's favorite dessert?
A: Vanilla Ice.

Kellen Brooks

Q: What do you call an angry snowman?
A: Water, because he's heated.

Q: Whats a snowman's favorite Christmas song?
A: Freeze-Navidad

Q: What snowmen had an incredible R&B career back in the day?
A: The Ice-ly Brothers.

Snowmen rarely fall in love. It melts their hearts.

I asked a snowman why he married so fast. He said "Its better to marry than to burn."

Jack Frost is gonna catch these hands if he keeps nipping at my nose!

Snowman Humor

I was about to tell you a new snowman joke. Then I froze.

I met a mean snowman. He's always cold.

Meteorologists rarely laugh. They have a cold front.

10
SPORTS HUMOR

I've got a movie idea about a guy and a girl that fell in love playing basketball then they moved in together while they were dating. It's called Shaq Up.

James doesn't like to wear dress shoes. He prefers Jim shoes.

Q: Why are scuba divers are the best philosophers?
A: Because the conversation is always deep.

Sports Humor

The pro golfer took everyone to school on the green! He used his bus driver.

The mailman saw me and said "put up your dukes!" He wanted to mail box.

I purchased a gym membership the other day. It hasn't been working out for me.

The bowling ball was very nervous, he's on pins and needles all the time.

The Olympic speed walker is now a motivational speaker. He encourages people to keep putting one foot in front of the other.

I met a mountain climber the other day. His name is Cliff.

I've got a movie idea about a dog that plays basketball really well. It's called Charles Barkley.

11
A LITTLE BIT OF EVERYTHING

Car Humor

Q: What's a mechanics favorite show?
A: Car-toons.

Q: Did you notice something about shy drivers?
A: They always drive the speed timid.

Luxury cars do well in school. They're always at top of the class.

A Little Bit of Everything

I asked my boss if he could pick me up in a limo for work. He said that's a stretch.

Susie's car fell apart after her crash test. Seems like the teacher rigged it that way.

I failed my driving test but I did my best, so the teacher gave me a striver's license instead.

Alphabet Humor

Never say your Alphabets at night or else you'll P in the bed.

Q: What question does W want to know?
A: Y, Z?

Q: What letters of the alphabet go to school?
A: The ones in LMNtery.

Q: What letter of the alphabet is always barking?
A: The Q's.

Political Humor

Q: Which President helped the most people get jobs?
A: Abraham LinkedIn.

Q: What president has the largest amount of debt?
A: Bills Clinton.

Q: What's a nick name for a rich man named William?
A: Dollar Bill.

Q: What clothing does a lawyer wear to court?
A: A lawsuit

Q: Which President is really into landscaping?
A: George Bushes.

Q: How does a judge tie his necktie?
A: With a judge knot.

Random Humor

Pre-teens have a peculiar smell. It's their adole-scent.

I'm trying out a new barnyard scented cologne. It's called Farm fresh.

I snapped a picture the other day. Now I'm trying to put it back together.

We finally found an employee who's a good *match* for our company. He strikes a fire under everyone.

Kellen Brooks

My mom put me on punishment for dancing in the dirt. She said "no dirty dancing on my watch!"

Being friends with comedians is hard. They're always acting funny.

Did you know the sun and moon were siblings? But their attitudes are day and night.

My grass and I had a really bad argument, so I cut my grass off for good. It told me "I'll be back. You'll see!"

I wonder, do tall people prefer to live in condominiums or condimaximums?

My television set is very paranoid. It told me, "I've got a feeling that someone is always watching me!"

A Little Bit of Everything

I'm hiring a babysitter. It's hard to find a babystander.

I did a pedicure for the first time. It was a large feet, but I made it!

Q: Name a germ that parties hard?
A: Fun-gus

Q: Why was the waist intimidated by the pants?
A: Because they pulled up on him!

Q: Why don't pine cones change colors?
A: Because they're forever green.

Kellen Brooks

Q: What do you call your Dad's touchy, emotional brother?
A: Uncle Feel

Q: How do you resuscitate a liar?
A: A DeFib-ulator

Q: Where do mops love to vacation?
A: Floor-da

Forget the amusement park. I know the perfect place for some senseless fun. The confusement park.

Q: What did Mr. and Mrs. Everybody name their child?
A: Loddy Doddy Everybody.

A Little Bit of Everything

Q: If lips had children what would they be called?
A. Chaps.

Q: What do you call a glutinous plumber?
A: A plumb-full.

Q: What do you call an internet criminal?
A: A Dot Con.

Q: What do you call a big guy in skinny jeans?
A: A tight situation.

I have a procrastination joke to tell you. I'll tell you later.

My throat got scratchy while on the airplane. I guess you could say I had a soar throat.

Kellen Brooks

I got insulted by a bottle of mouthwash the other day. He said he was only joking, but I think he mint it.

I decided to take a vacation on Halloween. It was a trip or treat.

People are captivated by electronic screens all day. I say it's Computer Love.

Just finished watching the biggest loser. It was weighty!

The fisherman downsized his boat. He now rides a lil' yachty.

There's an author named Barry who never tells the truth in his books. He's a lie Barry.

A Little Bit of Everything

A guy stole some luggage and got caught. They pressed charges and now he has a suit case. He tried to defend himself in court, but he couldn't carry on. They took him to jail, and had to leave his personal items. His situation was a lot to unpack!

I saw a baby being carried across a busy street. He was held up in traffic.

I hate to admit it, but I walk all over my step-dad.

Q: What's a rude woman's favorite purse?
A: An Offendi Bag.

Q: What kind of purse does a woman who likes to fight carry?
A: Louis Baton.

Kellen Brooks

Q: Why do kids play with boxes?
A: Because they're card-bored.

Q: What do you call a person with sweaty hands?
A: Palm Springs.

Q: What's another name for a cold toddler?
A: Ice ice baby.

Q: What do you call a father who plays pranks on his kids?
A: A Trick Daddy.

Q: What do you call a 7 foot liar?
A: A Tall Tell.

A Little Bit of Everything

Q: What's the most redundant job?
A: A male man.

Q: Why doesn't little orphan Annie use doorbells?
A: Because it's a hard knock life.

Q: Do you know what indifferent means?
A: I don't care!

One of the hardest things to do is get up from an easy chair.

19 and 20 got in a fight. 21.

I invented a device to solve life's hard problems. It's called the Problo-matic.

Kellen Brooks

I confronted my garbage man the other day because he kept talking trash.

A comedian killed the stage the other day. He was charged with mans-laughter.

I don't take soda tablets. I prefer pop pills.

I purchased a new medicinal blanket to help me fall asleep. It's called NyQuilt.

The astronaut bumped his head getting out of the space ship. Now he's really seeing stars.

A Little Bit of Everything

12
WITTY WISDOM

Always remember, when garbage can't, trashcan.

A drink of spring water always puts a bounce in your step.

Strange, but wearing a birthday suit to a birthday party is a bad idea.

Witty Wisdom

It doesn't take much to please a microscope. It's the little things.

Keep your eyes on the forest. They are shady characters!

It's good to have a therapist that's a life guard, just in case you're drowning in despair.

Here's a hot take: Mercury is the closest planet to the sun.

Strange, but wearing a birthday suit to a birthday party is a bad idea.

A circus clown rose from the bottom ranks to the new CEO of a Fortune 500 company. When they asked him how he did it, he said "Ha! I laughed my way to the top!"

Kellen Brooks

Recycle your news papers. It's old news anyway.

Pregnant women are just confident, even though they're full of it.

If you're gonna have children, have twins. I hear they're twice as fun.

During cold a flu season, always keep a pair of cross trainers for your runny nose.

A house plant told me its secret to success: "Beleaf in yourself."

If you're dealing with negative people at home, change all your light bulbs red. It'll help them develop.

If hair is acting bad, get a perm. That'll set it straight!

Witty Wisdom

Keep a traffic light with you at all times. That way you can make people that are driving you crazy stop.

Honey is a good friend. It sticks with you

Having big hair really helps marital intimacy. It's an Afro-disiac.

No losers are allowed on won way streets.

If you're sick, instead of going to a doctor, go to an ant heal. It won't cost a mound of money either.

Try to avoid eating smoked candy. It'll give you a sugar high.

I hope you had as much fun reading this book as I had creating it. Keep on laughing and share the joy with someone else! You'll be the life of the party.

-Kellen Brooks

For more content, visit KellenBrooks.com.

www.ingramcontent.com/pod-product-compliance
Lightning Source LLC
Chambersburg PA
CBHW020950090426
42736CB00010B/1346